Website or Blog: 10 Fast And Easy Tips, Tricks & Tools That Massively Increase Sales & Profits

Jim Edwards

Website or Blog: 10 Fast And Easy Tips, Tricks & Tools That Massively Increase Sales & Profits

Copyright © 2010 by Jim Edwards

Limits of Liability / Disclaimer of Warranty:

The authors and publisher of this book and the accompanying materials have used their best efforts in preparing this program. The authors and publisher make no representation or warranties with respect to the accuracy, applicability, fitness, or completeness of the contents of this program for any purpose.

They disclaim any warranties (expressed or implied), merchantability, or fitness for any particular purpose.

The authors and publisher shall in no event be held liable for any loss or other damages, including but not limited to special, incidental, consequential, or other damages.

As always, the advice of a competent legal, tax, accounting or other professional should be sought.

The authors and publisher don't warrant the performance, effectiveness or applicability of any sites or resources listed in this book. All links and resources are for information purposes only and are not warranted for content, accuracy or any other implied or explicit purpose.

This manual contains material protected under International and Federal Copyright Laws and Treaties. Any unauthorized reprint or use of this material is prohibited.

Visit Us Online
www.AQuickReadBook.com™

At the **A Quick Read Book**™ website, you'll find:

Chapter Excerpts from selected New Releases

Original Author and Editor Articles

Audio Excerpts

Electronic Newsletters

Author Contact Information

Tools and Resources Center

Plus Much, MUCH More!

Bookmark the **A Quick Read Book**™

Website at
www.AQuickReadBook.com™

Meet The Author
About Jim Edwards

Jim Edwards, founder of Guaranteed Response Marketing, LLC, is an Internet expert, marketing entrepreneur, newspaper columnist, author, motivational speaker and elite mentor and coach.

Having gained personal and financial freedom for

himself and his family, he shares his proven strategies with self-motivated, hard-working people to help them attain personal and financial independence.
He has written and published dozens of ebooks, print books and hundreds of articles. Through his company, Jim has produced some 40 informational products on DVD and many more available in the latest electronic formats downloadable from the Internet.

Jim produces and hosts webinars on a weekly basis and has been a frequent guest speaker at numerous international Internet marketing seminars.

He offers the exclusive "Jim Boat" seminar, an intensive seven-day program integrated into a Caribbean cruise, an inspirational setting for focusing on ways to achieve success. In its third year, the 2009 Jim Boat included over 100 participants from six countries.

Jim's successes are most compelling because they stem from his true life story. From childhood Jim was always driven to succeed. Though he excelled as a young man in real estate and mortgage banking, Jim left the industry to launch his own business. In just a few short years, his business failed, he lost all he acquired, and he struggled to support his family and survive.

He developed a heart condition and landed in the hospital staring death in the face. Thereafter, he declared bankruptcy.

With only one way to go, Jim climbed his way up, up and up using his keen mastery of the Internet, a simple marketing strategy and hard, honest work.

Within two years he was financially stable and free. A prolific creator and writer, Jim constantly has several books and new products in development at any given time.

For Terri,

who always believed in me, even when I didn't.

For little Johnny & Eli James

who showed me the meaning of unconditional love.

For my parents, Pat & Dallas…

see, all that talking when I was a little kid
finally paid off!

Bulk Book Order & Customized Version Information

Most **AQuickReadBook.com** titles are available at special quantity discounts for bulk purchases for sales promotions, premiums, fundraising, gifts or educational use.

In other words, if you'd like to get a truckload of copies of this book (or even just a dozen or two) to hand out at an event, company function, or as gifts to your clients, we can help you out at a substantial discount over the cover price.

Just contact us at www.AQuickReadBook.com and we'll get you a quote.

Also, special customized / company specific versions or excerpts can be created to fit specific needs. So if you'd like to do something customized with this book, drop us a line and we'll discuss it with you.

Our goal is to help you get what you need and to help our authors help as many people as possible with their books.

For more information, please contact us at A Quick Read Book™ online at

www.AQuickReadBook.com

Table of Contents

Introduction

Hey, everybody who decided to read and get some great benefits from this Quick Read Book. Welcome to "10 Fast and Easy Tips, Tricks & Tools that Massively Increase Sales & Profits on Any Website or Blog."

With no further ado, we're just going to jump right in, because we've got lots to cover over the next several chapters.

What we're going to cover … we're going to go over why you should listen to me every once in a while. It's a good thing to remind people that I might be worth listening to. You never know.

How you increase sales and profits on a website or blog.

What is conversion and why it matters.

How you increase conversion rates.

Warnings about guru advice. (I wonder what that is.)

10 fast and easy tips, tricks and tools you can use right now to increase sales & profits on any website or blog.

And of course, much, much more.

First, before we get started, I want to let you know the results of a quick poll I once took. The question I wanted to know the answer to was, "Do you have your own unique product to sell?"

I fired up the poll and got everybody to answer it.

The question is "Do you have your own unique product to sell?" The answers are "Yes and I'm making a killing with it." "Yes, but it's not doing much for me." "Yes, but it's not good quality." "No, but I sure want one." Or "No, I don't see a need to have my own product."

Go ahead and cast your vote.

We got about 55% of the vote in. That's good. We didn't want to spend a lot of time on the poll. We did a little countdown, five, four, three, two, one.

Let's close that up and let's take a look at the results. We have 1% saying "Yes and I'm making a killing with it."

39% say "Yes, but it's not doing much." 5% "Yes, but it's not good quality." 50%.

So half of the people here want a product and don't have one. And 4% say "No, I don't see any reason to have my own product."

I think that's very interesting, with everything that's going on in the world. We're going to talk about tips and tricks to increase sales, but half the people don't even have a product yet.

Why would I ask this when we're talking about increasing sales? Well, because a key to this whole process is your having a unique product that gives people a reason to buy from you and only you. Because one of the ways to get people to buy, or motivated actually, is exclusivity. You're the only source, so therefore, if they want to buy it, they can only buy it from you.

Having your own product is a really major building block on the sales and conversion platform.

The bottom line, despite what anybody tells you, you can only go so far as somebody else's affiliate. You need your own unique offer. If you look at the people out there selling "How to make money as an affiliate," what do they sell? They sell a product on how to make money as an affiliate.

If you pin them down, put them in a chokehold, raise your fist and said "What's making you more money?" I flat out guarantee you, they're making more money selling their product on how to be an affiliate, than they're making as an affiliate.

You've got to have your own unique product so that you can make your own unique offer. That's key.

Why listen to me? Why would you want to listen to Jim Edwards? Well, a few reasons, especially in the context of what we're talking about right here.

First, I've sold millions of dollars online in multiple markets, real estate, mortgage, typing, dog stuff. I do "How-to" on the Internet. Everything from how to make a website all the way on up, I've done it in multiple markets and multiple niches.

All my sales have been done online with sales letters, video, audio and opt-in offers. This is not like I went door-to-door. It's not like I did it through mail order.

I've been selling online since 1997, when I started selling my first eBook on How to Sell Your House Yourself. And the funny thing, almost 14 years later, that eBook is still selling with very little change.

I've been full time in my own online business since 2001. There's an interesting story behind that, we won't get into. But the reason I went full time is because I got fired from my off line job.

I have hundreds of thousands of subscribers and tens of thousands of satisfied customers on every single continent. And I really don't know how many countries, but I'd say it's well over 100.

 I have a proven track record of teaching and mentoring others to online success.

That's why you should listen to me.

Increasing Sales and Profits
On Websites and Blogs

Now, how do you increase sales and profits on a website or blog? And if you've got a website or blog this is a key question. You're going to want the answer, so here's the answer.

There are really only 2 ways, when it comes to your website. There are really only 2 ways to increase sales and profits. First, you sell more to people who come to your site. You increase sales conversions. If 100 people come to your site and you sell one, then you can double your revenue if you can figure out how to sell 2 instead of 1.

The other way is to increase the amount of purchase people make, when they actually buy, with either up-sales or suggestive selling. An up-sale is when somebody is going to buy something from you. Right before they buy, you say "hey, would you like to get this too?" That's called an up-sale.

The most famous example of that is "Would you like fries with that?" Because that's what McDonald's does. They make millions, if not billions a year just by saying, "Would you like fries with that?"

Suggestive selling is really a little bit different from up-sales, because that's where you're converting people to buy more, when they buy. Let's somebody's going to buy a dozen of something. You say "hey, if you'd like another dozen, we'll let you have that for 60% off" or 50% off.

A good example of a place that does this type of suggestive selling is Vistaprint. They will put you into what's called "up-sell hell," but they do a ton of suggestive selling in up-sales. It's a great thing to actually look at different examples of how people do that. That's www.vistaprint.com.

The bottom line, though, the easiest way to make more money is to increase conversion on either your initial sale or up-sells.

Another way to increase profit, a third way, is through reduced expenses. But if you increase conversion you're actually decreasing expenses as you go. We'll talk more about that later.

What is conversion and why does it matter? Conversion, simply stated, is the average number of people who buy the initial offer and/or the up-sell offer on your website or blog. Ultimately it's expressed as a number, usually as a percentage.

Again, if 1 out of every 100 people comes to your website and buys, you have a 1% conversion rate. Usually you should know the conversion rate of your website, down to at least 1/10 of 1%. So normally you'd say, I have a conversion rate of 1.3% or 7.6%.

I wouldn't worry too much about going to 1/100's of a percent, though you can. If you can just go to 1/10 of 1% that's enough until we start getting into huge numbers. That includes huge sale amounts, sale volume dollar amounts or huge numbers of people showing up to the website, thousands of visitors. Until then, only worry about it down to about 1/10 of 1%.

Normally when you increase conversion you don't in-crease cost, therefore, you instantly boost profits. That's what I alluded to earlier. So if you increase revenue and you keep your costs steady, then you're automatically going to make more profit. You can do that easily, just by increasing the conversion rate of your website.

That's what the 10 things we're going to talk about a little bit later are all about, increasing conversion.

Increasing Conversion

How do you increase conversion rate?   You do it simply by testing different things on your website or blog. You see which things make people buy or subscribe. We're going to talk about specific things at length, shortly.

You test, and there's a lot of information around on the Internet about testing. Usually it's put out there by people I'll call, the super geek set. I guess 50 years ago they'd call them the slide rule set.

These are the super geeks. They start using all kinds of words, verbiage, terms, nomenclature and what have you, that is just very confusing.   And it makes them feel important, because they can see the look on your face. You really don't know what they're talking about, so obviously you need their help.

The bottom line with testing, you measure two different variations of something across equal amounts of website visitors. That's testing. If you just did that, you would be doing more than the vast majority of people and you could massively increase your results.

For example, 100 people see Headline A and 100 people see Headline B and you measure the response differences between the two. Then you should be able to figure out which headline is going to perform better, worse or the same. If you just do that, then you're going to do really, really well.

That's testing in a nutshell.

The only 100% reliable way to increase conversion rate on any website or blog is to test different things on your website. Then you measure the results to see what works best. The kinds of results that you want to measure are really simple. And they all fall into one of several customer actions. That's an important thing to note.

It all comes down to customer action, because that's the most important thing you want to test on your website.

The results that we're looking for are phone calls generated from the web; customer e-mails from the web; customer contact through a form; subscriptions to a newsletter; clicks on a link and maybe an advertisement for an affiliate offer that we're making.

The best one of all is purchases through a website.

Your business may not be set up so you're worried about purchases through a website. Could be you're a real estate agent who needs to generate phone calls. That's how you measure the success or lack of success on your website.

The bottom line, it all comes back to results. And you need to know what percentage of people, who see a certain thing on your website, take a specific action as a result. That's your conversion rate and the way you increase it is to test different stuff.

Important To Beware

Now, it's very important for you to beware. I wish I had some horror music I could play for you right now, but I can't in a print book. But you need to beware... I want to share with you some things to beware of when testing and improving conversion on your website or your blog.

As I said, there's a ton of information going out there and testing and increasing sales has really devolved into a practice almost like voodoo. It's something that people want you to think is hard. They want you to think it is tough, so they can sell you some $5000 course.

The biggest things you need to beware of are the pronouncements of absolutes, when it comes to what works in sales conversion. Now what am I talking about? What are absolutes?

You need to be careful when gurus say things like "This works," or "This doesn't." And everybody adopts it as gospel. You'll see this in different little niches on the web, but especially when it comes to online business. You have some people who attain guru status. They are the cat's pajamas. They are "it." Whatever they say, by golly, that's the way it is.

You'll see these things start going around the web. And you'll see people copying people or people saying "This works," "This doesn't."

Some examples of that, red headlines don't work as well as blue headlines. Now this was huge a few years ago and it comes up here and there. You'll hear somebody say "Red headlines don't work." Or "Blue headlines don't work." Or "You should do a purple headline." Or "It should be in the form of a graphic with some sort of drop shadow on it." Or "It should have some sort of glow around it."

They'll say "That's the way headlines should be done. Those are the ones that work." Or you'll hear people say "You should never use a blue text link, you should always use a clickable button." Or this is another one that's really big right now "You should always use an orange Order button that says 'Next Page' on it. That's the one that will work." Or, "An eBook graphic always increases sales."

What happens, people start using this advice to the point where they get obsessive about it. They just get blown out of the water trying to remember, who said what about what. This doesn't work and it never works. They end up not even trying things that might work or might work better.

You've got to be really careful about some words that should make you nervous when you hear somebody say them. No matter if it's in an article or on a webinar or in person or at a seminar or on a sales letter. You need to be really careful whenever you see somebody say "always" or "never," or "right" or "wrong."

When it comes to increasing sales and profits on a website or blog it really comes down to this. The individual sales message comes down to the specific audience and it comes down to the specific offer. What might work in one spot may not work as well in another.

And what works poorly in one area might be the missing link to making millions of dollars in another. You just don't know. That's why we test, test, test, test.

Anytime you hear these words, when it comes to sales copy or conversion, et cetera, you need to ask yourself this question. When you hear "always" or "never" or "right" and "wrong," how do they know this? What is making them say this?

There's a book I really believe that everybody should read. It's called How to Lie With Statistics. It's available from leading internet retailers. It's less than $10.

It was written back in the 50's, and one of the most important books I've ever read in my life. It will show you that when people start throwing things around, there's more BS attached to statistics than anything else.

The people holding up a percentage and saying this is the justification for you to do something, are usually the ones with some sort of hidden agenda. You always want to know how do they know this and will this apply to my audience.

The answer is always-did you notice I'm using the word "always"-the answer is, always take with a grain of salt and test for yourself as soon as possible. That is the safest thing you can do, especially when you have a website that's working and you're tempted to make a wholesale change to it, just because somebody said that you should.

Or you're getting all stressed out about having every single thing perfectly right on your website or blog before you even get started. Here you get into paralysis of analysis because you can't even get started. You're too busy trying to make sure that you're crossing every T, dotting every I and following the advice of every guru.

The only things that you can or should take as gospel truth, are the things you actually prove yourself on your own website or blog. That's really the only thing that you can know as an absolute, when it comes to your sales message going out to your audience to sell your product, using the sources of traffic that you're generating.

You want to test as much as you can, but you want to keep it simple and easy. I've seen too many people get freaked out by this whole process. They end up not being able to take any consistent or good action whatsoever.

Remember, one of the fastest ways to increase profits online is to increase your conversion. If you take nothing out of this first section of the book, it's this main point. You should probably write this down in the blank pages provided.

One of the fastest ways to increase profits online is to increase your conversion.

Instead of looking for magic sources of traffic or the magic whatever, if you can just bump your conversion a little bit, it can make a huge difference in your business.

Okay, now let's dive into the 10 fast and easy tips, tricks and tools you can use right now to increase sales and profits on any website or blog.

Google's Free Website Optimizer Tool

The first one is to use Google's free Website Optimizer Tool. This is by far and away, the best free tool ever, to increase online sales. If you're looking for answers, I can imagine questions. I can imagine readers asking "Okay, well, how do I test? How do I measure?"

This is how you test and this is how you measure A/B things on your website. The Website Optimizer Tool is available at www.adwords.google.com. In order to find it, the funny thing is that they buried it. It's like the most valuable thing they have and Google chose to bury it.

What you have to do is log into your AdWords account and the new interface. You click on Opportunities, then you click on Optimize Your Website. That's how you get to it. They've got really good tutorials in there, so I'm not going to go into the mechanics of using it in this book, because they've got videos that show you how to do it.

This is free with your Google AdWords account. What it does is let you test multiple variables and pick a winner.

Nine times out of 10 I simply use it for just doing A/B split testing. Testing one price against another; testing one headline against another; testing a set of bullets against another. Use it testing with or without a video versus another; or testing a background color; or testing the width of something. I'll talk more about results a little later.

This software used to cost thousands of dollars to get the same software set up, and now it's free with opening a Google AdWords account for $5.

Literally this happened. This was the software to use and so Google wanted people to get better results and spend more money with Google AdWords, which is their Pay Per Click service. So they bought it and offered it for free. If you can increase conversion you'll probably increase your spending on Google AdWords, which makes them billions. It keeps the owners as billionaires and the world keeps spinning on its axis, as it should.

This is really the tool the pros use to test and measure conversion. There are others out there, but I would tell you, this is what I use. This is what all my buddies use. And this is what you should use. You can do both A/B split tests and multi-varied testing.

Multi-varied is where you would change like 4 things on the website all at once. Then it would figure out the best combination of all 4. The negative from doing that, it can take what seems forever to get results.

That's not really helpful when you might only be getting a couple hundred visitors a day or 100 visitors a day or 300 visitors a day. You can't get enough traffic in a fast enough period of time to declare one set a winner. I would rather do A/B like I described before.

Here's an example of an A/B split test we did. This was actually testing with and without video at the top of a sales page. I want to point out that we were testing with the video at the top and then without the video.

With the video it converted at 2.08%. Without the video it converted at 1.84%.

That may not sound like a big difference, but when you're selling a $1000 product, 8 more sales translates to $8000. It was definitely worth testing this, because then moving forward we're able to use the version that's going to convert the best.

Video, like I said, converted at 2.08%; without video it converted at 1.84%. You might say okay, .24% really isn't something to get really excited about. But if you look at the percentage of the percentage, a .24% increase is actually 13% more sales. That's a 13% increase over 1.84%.

When you're talking about spending money to get traffic, a 13% increase in sales could actually represent a 30%, 40%, 50% or even more percentage increase in profit. Look when you're spending $90 to make $100 in sales. All of a sudden for every $90 you spend, you can make $120. That means, instead of making $10 for every time you spend $90, you're making $30, which actually represents a 300% increase in profit.

That's why, being able to measure this is so important.

The Google Website Optimizer Tool is something you need to become very, very familiar with and start using. You can use it on a regular website and on a blog.

Test Headlines First And Often

Now, the next tip is to test headlines first and often. This is your highest leveraged activity once you start selling. Once you have a sales process online that's actually working, where you're actually making sales, you're driving traffic. You're converting people to buyers and you have a closed loop where it's actually working, then testing headlines is key.

Every single web page or blog post should have a headline, because that lets people know instantly what the page or post is about. And that way they know whether it's something they should pay attention to or they should move on to something else.

Just as an example, imagine a newspaper with no headlines. I wrote for a newspaper for 11 years. I was a syndicated newspaper columnist. The first thing that the editor would always look at was not the article or the conclusion, they would always look at the headline. Because that's going to let them know what people are going to be interested in. And a great headline is what pulls people in.

A crap article or a crappy blog post or crappy sales letter with a great headline, is going to always outsell a great article, blog post or sales letter, which has a bad headline. That's why you really want to test headlines first.

The fastest tests that you can do are completely different headlines, so that's where you would do an A versus B. You might do "How Any New Parent Can Raise a Happy Child" versus "Make Your Child an Einstein." They're two completely different headlines. You're just looking to see which one is going to get you more sales, is going to grab people.

Once you've got a headline that's doing pretty well, then you want to start doing tweaking headline tests. One of the fastest ways to do those is to try framing them.

An example would be "How to Raise a Happy Child" versus "How You Can Raise a Happy Child", Or "How to Improve Your Tennis Stroke" versus "How You Can Improve Your Tennis Stroke."

Those sound very similar but they have a completely different frame. One has got "you" in it. And one is all about them. The other is not about them. And you will see differences.

Again, see if you've got something that's working, something that's converting at 2%. Then you can, just with a
simple tweak, get it to go to 2.1% or 2.2% or 2.3%. All
of a sudden you're talking about a 10% increase in
conversion just with a simple change.

Those are the two best types of headline tests to make.
Either completely different, A/B, or tweaking the framing
of the actual headline.

Some other things you can test with headlines. Once
you've found one that works you're going to want to test
color, you're going to want to test size and you're going to
want to test font. Whether it's red, blue, green, purple,
whatever. Whether it's 14 point, 18 point, 24 point, and
whether it's Arial or Times New Roman. This can make a
big difference once you've found a headline that works.

Just as an aside, I've seen changes in testing headlines.
I've seen one headline change increase conversion for me
personally by over 400% in less than 10 minutes. I was
doing a product launch for a new audio CD product. I
had a headline that was very centered on me. It was how
I did this and how I did that, how I gained an unfair
advantage in life and how I started living the life of my
dreams.

I reframed it to how "you" can get an unfair advantage in life and start living "your" dreams. That reframe, as soon as I changed it, saw a 400% increase in sales.

That's pretty cool when you see it happening. Then you want to kick yourself when you think about all the sales that you missed. But we let that go.

To Click or Not To Click, That Is The Question

The third thing we want to talk about is, to click or not to click. That is the question. Clickable buttons versus text. What you want to do is test using purchase buttons versus blue underlined text.

These would be examples of the two different ones. The one on top is actually a button like you would see on a form. Somebody could click that and that takes them through to the, in this case Shopping Cart. Or, beneath it, blue underlined clickable text, which actually looks kind of purple. So there you go.

Or after reading this example, if you do a test yourself in black and white, take my word for it, it's blue underlined. It says "Click here now to download your copy."

There are some people who will swear that one is better than the other. I'm here to tell you that one is not automatically better than the other. You need to test it.

Another thing to test is outlining the button, versus not outlining it. On the left you would see it's outlined in red to grab people's attention. When somebody runs their mouse over the top of it, it will turn green so they know that they're supposed to click. Then you would see an example over here where there's nothing surrounding it.

I've seen situations where one works better than the other. I can't tell you the circumstances, because all I can tell you is you need to test it. But again, these are the kinds of things you would test after you've tested headline and price, things like that.

Some experts say people want click buttons, others say they want to click blue underlined text. The real answer, like I said, is to test. But it can make a real difference in conversion either way.

It's interesting, because I fell into a trap. A guru was running around saying "Oh, you've got to use a button. Button is the only thing that's going to work. Only thing that's going to work." Blah, blah, blah, blah, blah.

I said I'm going to use a button. Well then a friend of mine said "Maybe we should test a clickable link just for the heck of it." In this particular case, on this particular site, the clickable link massively outperformed the clickable button. And I've seen vice versa as well. So it just depends again on the audience, the offer, traffic, all that. You've got to test it.

The Words You Use Matter

No. 4, the words you use where they click, matter. What you need to do also is test the text on your button or in your link.

I've seen using just one different word, using the word "my" versus the word "your" on a link has increased conversion by as much as 15%. And that's on an Order link or on a Subscription button.

I found that the best default text to start with, actually starts with two words, "Click here." So do this, if in doubt of what to put on an Order link or on a button. You can't normally go wrong with this as the first stuff that you put on there.

"Click here for" whatever. "Click here for my free webinar registration."

I found the following results through extensive testing and told them to a group of people who attended one of my webinar presentations live on this approach and choice. You clicked a button that said "Click here for my free webinar registration." And I have found in this particular situation that saying "Click here for my free webinar registration" outperforms "Click here for your free webinar registration." And having either one of those, normally outperforms, "Click here for free webinar registration."

The "my" seems to win most of the time in this situation. And I do it 3 or 4 times, or 2 or 3 times or even if it just totally kicks butt just 1 time. I just make that the default of how I do stuff. As long as my overall conversion rate just keeps going up and up and up with other things I test, then I don't worry too much about going back and retesting stuff.

What you also want to do is test a benefit statement or end result in your text or button. Again, "Click here for benefit." "Click here to get your free eBook." "Click here now to download your copy."

That seems to be a really good starting point. When you're figuring out what text to put in a link or in a button, use "Click here" to get a benefit. "Click here for a free webinar registration." "My free webinar registration." "Click here now to download your copy."

In this case it wouldn't make sense to say "Click here now to download my copy." But it makes perfect sense to say "Click here now to download your copy." And I've tested this back and forth, "Click here now to download," "Click here now to download your copy." And in this particular web page, in this particular offer, "Click here now to download your copy" outperformed that.

On With The Show...

No. 5, and now on with the show. Some old time TV gives clues for successful video production in the 21st Century. We have found that videos can boost your sales and opt-ins significantly. Video is proven to help increase sales. However, you need to test it for your audience, to see how they react.

It may help you increase sales and subscribers. And in other cases it may kill your response. And not kill in the show biz sense of, "You killed it," but in the dead animal on the side of the road, "you killed it." You need to be very, very careful about making pronouncements.

My overall finding is that video helps.

Some specific tips when it comes to video. Short versus long, in this case you want to default to short. One test I didn't share with you because it was relatively inconclusive. It was on the previous thing where we talked about the sales letter with the video at the top, versus not with video.

We had a pretty long video and we had a pretty short video and it was pretty even which one was converting better than the other. Since one wasn't really beating the other one, we just defaulted to the short one.

The thing with video, there's so much information communicated with it that 5 minutes can seem like an eternity. If you have a choice between a 5-minute video and a 2-minute video, start with the 2-minute video and then start testing different videos.

Another thing about videos, you want to keep it very simple and direct. Tell people exactly what to do. Even to the point of pointing, literally pointing with your finger and telling them to put in their name and e-mail address. You can even tell them to click the button.

"Hey, I'm Jim Edwards. Go ahead, put in your name and primary e-mail address right over here. Click the button. And then go check your e-mail to get the special report."

Or, point and tell them to click the link to get started. "I'm Jim Edwards. Go ahead, scroll down the page. Click the button and we'll see you on the other side and get started."

Literally they see you pointing. You can't see me point-ing right now of course, but imagine I'm pointing my finger and telling them what to do. Just keep it very simple and direct, if you're not real experienced with making video. That's a way that you can do better with your video over someone who just rambles and rambles.

Also what you want to do is avoid generalizations about video. Because video is so popular, because video is such a big deal, because video is the thing that everybody's talking about. Everybody has a new service online or is looking to get venture capital or get Google to buy them. Everybody is saying video, video, video, video. It's the only thing. Everything is about video now.

You'll see other people on the other end saying "Aw, video is limited and doesn't work." You'll find this instead, especially when you make your first video. If you just go and wing it, you need to ask yourself, is my video not working? Does that mean videos suck or does it mean that your video sucks?

You've got to be careful about any generalizations like that. Does your audience have a high speed connection?

That would be the first thing I would ask. Does your audience have a high speed connection? And are they interested in watching video.

Just because billions of people are watching videos, maybe 80% of them are teenagers watching skateboard videos. I don't know. It depends on your audience.

Another thing you've got to think about, especially if you're selling to business market. Are people who would see your video, at work where they can't have their speakers turned up? So if they hear sound, they're going to bail immediately. They pull up to a website, they don't expect video. All of a sudden you start screaming about buy, buy, buy, buy, and they're going to bail.

It might be that video is just not appropriate for your particular audience. Or the way you made your video is not particularly good. You've just got to be careful about making those generalizations. The biggest thing you can do is just keep it simple, keep it direct and tell people exactly what to do with your video.

If It Works For Late-Night Infomercials...

No. 6 tip, if it works for late night infomercials then it's good enough for all of us. Here are some tips for increasing your online video effectiveness. There are 3 of them where you really can't go wrong by giving them a try. Video can be improved no matter how boring the topic.

The first way to do is to add appropriate music. Appropriate means it makes sense. If it's a happy, upbeat topic, then you have happy music and upbeat music. If it's a serious topic, then you have somber, serious music. You want to make sure you only use royalty free music.

A buddy of mine, Mike Stewart, has a website where he sells royalty free music at www.twodollarthemes.com. Mike composes it all himself and it's really good. And that's all we use. When people are on one of my webinars or they listen to a CD or DVD, we're using royalty free music. That is key.

You cannot take your latest Randy Travis album and lift some music out of it and expect to be able to use it and not get in any trouble. Even though you see people doing that on YouTube, they shouldn't be doing it. With your luck you'll be the one that gets sued by ASCAP, so don't do that. Only use royalty free music.

The other thing you can do with video is to add text overlays. Text overlays are where you see text in addition to full motion video. Or text can be just the whole video. You can make a whole video just with a black screen and white text on it. As long as you've got some music and good narration, it could still be exciting or emotional. All kinds of stuff you can do.

The great thing about text overlays, it hits people on multiple levels when you use this. People see you, they hear you, they read the text and you can show examples. You can also do so many different things, but you're reinforcing it with their seeing you, seeing your emotion, hearing you talk, hearing the tone of your voice, seeing the text on the screen. And it also lets you control their focus, because words reinforce key message points.

If I'm narrating something people see the main keywords or the main thought in text. The whole time on there it keeps them focused and it gives them something else to look at.

The third thing you can do to increase your online video effectiveness is to remember that every single video ends with a specific call to action. If you go look at most of the videos out there on the web, you will see that most of them do not have a specific call to action.

You need to tell people at the end of your video, tell them what to do. Tell them what to think. Tell them where to go next. Most people's videos leave the viewers hanging. And you don't want to be like them. They're looking to be led by your video. They watched it, they're looking to get something out of it, unless you're doing something just designed to make them laugh or to be humorous.

Even if you accomplish that, if you get them to laugh, then you get them to have enough level of interest. Then they are excited about it enough to laugh or get mad or whatever, then tell them "Hey, would you like more of this? Go to my blog and sign up." "Go to my website and sign up."

You'll be amazed just with those 3 changes to your video, adding music, adding text overlays and adding a call to action at the end of every single video. You will be amazed at the increase in not only response, but in conversion that you get from using video.

Make Their Pot Boil Over...

No. 7, Make their pot boil over. How to build effective, ethical pressure to make a purchase decision.

The way you make their pot boil over is build pressure to act with bullets. Now what are bullets? Bullets are used in either sales copy, e-mail teasers, video scripts. They're used to tell people what you have to offer, but they give details without giving away the secret or the answer. Especially, in the case of information products.

The bottom line with bullets is that they build desire and curiosity. If you go look at anything, look at the back of a book. You'll see bullets that are designed to make you excited about what's in the book. But they don't necessarily tell you exactly what it is. Same thing with a DVD. Same thing with a car. Same thing with a TV ad. They're little chunks of information designed to build desire and curiosity. And they're done in short, pithy little snippets that get you excited.

The No. 1 mistake that people make with bullets that kills, or should I say destroys online sales and profit? It does nothing to help with your conversion unless you are selling to a group of engineers. The No. 1 mistake people make with bullets is having the wrong focus.

When most people are putting together a sales message on their blog or on their website, they talk about Features when they list off the bullets. A Feature is what something is.

What's an example of that? "Our tennis rackets are made from graphite resin for added stiffness." That's what something is.

Some people, especially if you let the R&D department write your marketing material, would think "Wow, graphite resin, that gives added stiffness." What they're doing is assuming that the person reading that feature can figure out what is in it for them. Why they should care in the first place.

Again, if you're buying software or some sort of mechanical something, at some point features are going to be important in an evaluation process. It's hard to use a feature to get somebody excited, especially when we're talking about sales messages and increasing sales and profits on our website or blog.

The next thing, some people instead of talking about features, talk about benefits, when they list off bullets. In fact, talking about bullets as far as benefits, is really what most sales copy training focuses on. It's features and benefits, features and benefits, features and benefits.

You've probably heard that before. A benefit is what something does or, it's what a feature does. An example would be "Our tennis rackets give you 25% more power with the same stroke and creates much more power for the same energy."

Okay, well that's a little bit more exciting. That's better than, it's real stiff. Maybe I don't like a stiff racket. But this, okay, more power. That sounds kind of good. Same stroke, more power. There you go.

The real tip, though, the real thing with using bullets is to build pressure. Very few people talk about it and very few people teach it, and very few people even know to do it. When you're writing sales copy you want to talk about what a feature or benefit means to the person who's reading it. Actually, if you can use all three, that can be very, very helpful.

A Meaning is what you want to really talk about in a lot of your bullets when you're looking to increase sales and profits.   Meaning is how something impacts people's lives.

To continue the tennis racket example, you might have a bullet that says "Our racket's graphite composite gives you a more powerful stroke, which gives you the edge over your rivals during the next club championship."

Think about that. If you're buying a tennis racket, you're not buying a tennis racket because it's stiff. You might be buying it so it will give you a more powerful stroke. But the ultimate reason that you're buying a tennis racket, it will help you win. Tennis is not like golf which is a lot more social. Tennis, unless you're playing doubles, tennis is more like a duel.

Tennis you want to beat the other person. And you beat them in direct combat. That's why there's not that much business discussed on the tennis court as opposed to the golf course. But I digress.

The bottom line is if you can tell people what a feature and benefit actually means to them.   You're going to do much, much better when it comes to actually converting them into a sale.

The thing to remember is make sure that your bullets address what I call WIIFM. Actually I call it that, but somebody else called it that first. And that's "What's in it for me?" You want to talk in terms not only of what your product does, but in terms of the benefits and how those benefits impact the lives of your readers, listeners and viewers.

You can't talk exclusively in terms of features or just benefits or just meaning. You have to use all of them. But by using all of them you're going to do much, much better than if you just concentrate on one.

If it's just features, then you're only going to appeal to the analytical people. Analytical is really… not that many people make buying decisions based just on being ana-lytical.

If you only talk in terms of benefits, then the people who need some more information about how something works, aren't going to be able to make that decision.

And if you talk only in terms of meaning, then you're going to come off as hypey, and so you've got to have a mix of all three.

Does Size Really Matter?

Tip No. 8. Does size really matter? Yes, it does, ladies and gentlemen. Let's talk about long sales copy versus short sales copy, if you want to sell anything to anyone, online especially. You are ultimately going to come head-to-head, butt your head up against the argument of long copy versus short sales copy.

You'll hear all the arguments in between. "It doesn't work in my market." "It won't work in that market." "Oh, they'll never read that much copy. They're into pictures." You hear all this different... and people can dig in their heels about it. You hear all sorts of different philosophies about it.

People make snap judgments about copy as either too long or short. And it's important to remember that what you want to do is get people to absorb your sales message. In order to get them to absorb your sales message, you have to give them enough information to make a decision without going overboard.

There's no such thing as long sales copy unless your sales copy sucks. And I think that there's been a real tendency towards long copy, because that comes out of laziness or lack of knowledge.

Mark Twain had a really cool quote. He said "I didn't have time to write a short letter so I wrote a long one." He meant that it actually takes a lot more thought, a lot more skill to write a short, effective message, than it does just to ramble on and on and hope that you've hit all the bases.

I will say this on a lot of these sales letters you'll see online that are 40 or 50 pages long. They seem to be in this endless cyclical going over the same stuff. Didn't I just read that about 18 inches above in the sales copy? That's laziness. That's not effective sales copy. You want to be very careful about emulating that type of writing.

You just want to make sure you get to the point and tell people what they need to know. Long enough is long enough. And don't fall victim to some prescription about how long or short something should be.

There are formulas for what elements should be in a sales letter. Things like prime, agitate, solve, guarantees, price, price drop and PS. It's important to learn about those things. But you can also have a situation where you use that formula and each part is one or two sentences. It doesn't have to be that each part is 3 pages long. That's another trap that people fall into.

What you want to do is just target your audience well and write directly to them. Give them the information they need to make a decision.

Let me give you an example. This one really should make you sit up and think. We had two variations of a sales letter that we were sending people to. This was for a $1000 product. We had one variation that had a 16% conversion rate; and another variation that had a 10.5% conversion rate. Again, this was a $1000… well, okay, $997 product. Let's just call it $1000.

Big difference in sales numbers here. I'd love to have this conversion rate on everything I ever do. "Oh, man, our sales conversion rate is only 10.5%. I'd much rather have everything be 16%." But this was a $1000 product and the difference between 36 sales at one level and 47 sales is pretty significant.

Oh, and by the way, the variation that won was the long version. In fact, it was 5 times longer. But the thing is, I've seen them where you've had similar results where it was flipped. The short sales copy massively outperformed the long sales copy, specifically in the area of optIn offers and free webinar offers. But also in the area of sales offers.

The only way you can know for sure is to test. In this case the long one won. It was almost a 50% increase in sales. But like I said, in other cases I've seen the short copy win. You can't prejudge, you have to test.

Does This Make Me Look Fat?

Tip No. 9 is does this make me look fat? "Now be honest, does this make me look fat?" This one I discovered by accident, in adjusting the page width and background colors of a website, specifically a sales letter website. I literally really did discover this by accident.

The background color of your page can affect conversion rate. It affects people physically or subconsciously. I'm not sure why. But in the background, the color of your website, especially the background color, and typically the way we make websites or blogs, we have a white page. Then it's a specific width in the middle centered and then you'll have either white or some other color or an image behind.

Most people don't give it any thought. They just either do it by default or they do something they think looks cool. Whenever you're doing something just because you think it looks cool, that's an internal cue this is something you might want to test. I don't know why the color of your background on your page can affect conversion rate, but I know it has a measureable effect, because I've tested it multiple times.

Like I said, I found this out by accident on the payment processor that I was using on a particular website. They changed their page colors and the payment processor was ClickBank. I have multiple, many websites using ClickBank. What happens is you have the sales letter on your website. They click a button and they go over to ClickBank's website.

They leave your website and they go to ClickBank's website. They changed the page color, the background page color. And my conversions went down significantly. They went down more than 25%. Just one day, sales were down.

After a week I was like damn, my sales are down this week. I wonder what's going on. Then another week went by and they stayed down. I said I haven't changed anything, I haven't changed… I haven't changed anything.

I went and looked and I clicked on the Order button and I went to their site and it was like a smack in the face. It was obvious that people had left my site and they had gone somewhere else. It looked so different from my website. I could see how people would go "Oh, I don't understand what's going on here. I'm just going to leave."

What I did was change the background color of my page-originally the background color was white-to match theirs and conversions went back up. Now it doesn't match exactly, I guess they've been doing some experimentation as well. But it's close enough so when you click on this link and you go over here to their website, it doesn't really look like you've left my site.

That's critical, this is something ultimately you've got to test? I can't tell you whether… and this is another thing where you'll hear gurus say "Oh, white, it's got to be white." Or "Never use black." Or "Always use navy blue." Or "It should always have a drop shadow and rounded corners."

I say BS. What I say is, you've got to test it yourself.

Another thing you can do, I decided to test this on a webinar offer. I said okay, well this happened on a sales page. I wonder if this will influence people subscribing or actually opting in for an offer for a webinar. I did a background color, as the only variable that was different, among 3 different versions of the sales page.

I tested the original that was white and then we tested navy blue and we tested black. The white got a conversion rate of 55.7%, the black got 58.9% and the blue got 59.2%. We ran almost 4500 visitors here, so this is statistically significant for this particular offer.

What happened was the blue outperformed the other. It increased from 55.7% to 59.2%. The weird thing, though… and that's a 6.2% increase if you look at the difference based on the original number. The other interesting thing, that didn't always hold true for every single webinar offer. I don't know why. It just didn't.

What I found is to pretty much just use the white background, because I had another experiment, where the dark blue massively underperformed the white. So depending on what I'm doing, normally I'll just do the white. But it meant that 6 more people out of every 100 opted in, for this particular case.

Another thing I did, we called it a what-the-hell-why-not test. This actually did influence stuff that we've done since then in a big way. We decided to test page width, the width of the table that everything was in. We tested a table that was 770 pixels wide versus… pretty much everything we had been doing up 'til then was 600 pixels wide.

Years ago the average browser resolution was 800 pixels by 600 pixels. When you had a 600 pixel wide table in the middle, you had about 100 pixels on either side, a little less because the sidebar takes up room. But it looked nice, centered in the middle of somebody's web browser.

The average default resolution went up from 800 to 600 to 1024 by 768, so at 600 pixels wide it looks pretty narrow in there. I'm not saying this will hold true all the time, but it can look kind of narrow. By widening it, we wanted to see if that would make a difference.

What happened was we tested 600 versus 770. The difference in conversion was 6.25% for 600 versus 7.26% at the 770. So basically, over 1% difference. Again, this was not a small dollar product. I think it was a $500 product.

Big difference in sales, especially when you start talking about thousands of visitors, just by having it a little bit wider and I guess making it easier for people to read. So the 770 increased sales conversion by over 1%. But that's a 16% increase in sales. But again you're looking at keeping costs level, especially when you're buying traffic, paying for traffic. Google AdWords or things like that, article traffic, things like that, a 16% increase in sales could double your profitability.

Anyway, that's another thing that's definitely worth testing. You don't want to get caught up thinking that one thing is right over another and you want to pay attention to these different areas that you can test. Because I was frankly shocked at the difference in sales, with that being the only difference.

Before You Go...

Now, tip No. 10 is one more very important thing before the end of this book . This is a last ditch effort to make that sale when people are at your website. What you want to do is start making exit offers. An exit offer is an offer you make to people when they leave your site. That might sound basic, but hardly anybody does this anymore. Or if they do it, they do it wrong.

What you want to do is use an exit script that pops an offer when people leave. Let me tell you basically how that works.

Somebody comes to your website or blog and they click around and they look at various pages and whatnot. Then they say "Well, I'm not interested in this". "This isn't what I was thinking about," or any of 100 different reasons they leave.

As soon as they either hit their back button or they hit the X button at the top of the page, a good exit script is going to pop some sort of an offer. This can come either through a light box or through a Java script warning dialogue box or both. It's basically going to make them an offer with some text right here and a couple of buttons. One will say "Okay" and one will say "Cancel." People's normal inclination is to hit what? Cancel.

When you hit Cancel, that leaves you on the exit page with the exit offer. Hardly anybody hits Okay, because Okay would mean wait a minute, what's going on here? I'm either going to hit Cancel or I'm going to hit the X button, which is exactly what you want them to do with a good exit script.

Then you make them some sort of an exit offer. An exit offer is a perfect way to make money, get subscribers or to gather marketing intelligence. Those are the 3 things that you want to do.

One exit offer that you can make is to offer people free information. If you offer them free information you're trying to capture them as a subscriber. Then you can market to them through e-mail over time.

Here's an example. "If you leave my website without buying I'm going to offer you a free eBook mini-course." It says "Click Cancel, get our 4-part mini-course free on how you can publish an eBook bestseller." This offers them something that they want. We've gotten thousands of subscribers doing that. Whereas, if we didn't have that, then they would leave.

Next thing you can do is offer a down-sell. A down-sell is where you offer a version of the product at a lower price or you offer them an alternative of some kind. "Hey, if you're not interested in this, then maybe you'd be interested in this and it's not nearly as expensive."

Some people use this in a very, I'm going to say, non-ethical way. They use it in a cheesy way; in a way that abuses people. They come to the website and then they leave. Then you offer them a half price offer on exactly what they would have just paid full price for. That doesn't make any sense. And if they find out they're going to be pissed.

A down-sell is where you take stuff away and then you can legitimately lower the price. One of the places we've used this very successfully is a product called "Five Steps to Getting Anything You Want" . That's $97 plus shipping and handling.

We offer a down-sell offer of the CD only for $29. The 5 steps… the $97 version has 2 CD's and a print workbook and another downloadable bonus that is worth way beyond $97. All that together, it's well worth that. But we do a down-sell offer of the CD only, no second CD, no downloadable bonus and no print workbook. $29 plus shipping and handling for the CD, it's enough of a distinction that no one's ever gotten mad.

What we do is when they leave without buying. We make them an offer that says "Wait, I'm going to give you over 70% off. You can get just the CD for $29 plus shipping and handling. Click Cancel now to find out more."

And I've also got an audio button that basically reads this. "For over 70% off as a special marketing test I'm offering you a full audio CD of '5 Steps to Getting Anything You Want' for only $29 plus shipping and handling. It doesn't include the second audio CD or the workbook, but it does include the entire audio program that's changed thousands of lives."

So we increased profit on that site by over 43%. That's a pretty cool exit offer.

Another thing that you can do is ask why they aren't buying or subscribing. Let's say you've put a bunch of time, energy and effort into putting up an offer. You've created a sales message, whether it's a video, sales letter, whatever.   And you're running that puppy out there and you're driving traffic and nobody's buying.

You're freaking out, because you've had 100 then 200 then 300 visitors. Nobody's buying. Well, crap. Why aren't they buying? The easiest way to find out why they aren't buying is to ask them.

I did this recently on an offer that I thought was great. I thought it was awesome. Again, you should stay and act very carefully on the advice of gurus. I had seen somebody saying this was the best thing since sliced bread, you should do this.   This was somebody a lot of people followed, paid attention to and he was making a good argument.

I said okay, let me give this a try. If it's good I'll give the guy credit. If it sucks, I won't.

I was getting ready to reorganize a whole portion of my business around this, because this person swore that this worked. I put together this whole offer. And it totally, totally bombed. It turns out that my customers thought that the offer really sucked. And it caused me really to re-evaluate a business decision that I'd made. It saved me from some major heartache and from going down a trail that would have been very costly.

It was actually the simplest of any of these exit offers. All I did was ask them a really simple question. And they will tell you what's wrong with your site and your offer. And then you can use that intelligence to change the offer and then increase your conversion rate.

In the case I just told you about, I made a very simple... I mean this took me about literally about 5 or 10 minutes. Because I was distraught, man. Seriously, I was distraught. I didn't understand why this wasn't working.

I put up a little page that says "Why?" "Why isn't this... Why?" Then the audio message basically said "Hey, I made what I thought was a killer offer. Would you mind just telling me why you're not taking advantage of it? I'd really appreciate your feedback."

Frankly, I got lambasted. I had people tell me "I can't believe you're making this kind of offer." "This is cheesy." "This sounds just like" so and so and so and so. I was like yeah, well they're the ones that I saw doing it, so I figured I'd give it a try. They really let me have it.

Again, it kept me from running down a rabbit hole.

Bottom line is you want to make exit offers. You literally are just figuratively or virtually tapping people on the shoulder as they're walking out the door from your website. You ask them for one last chance at a sale, some bit of information or even just a chance to sign up to your list.

Everybody concentrates, the other side of the coin, where I talked about increasing conversion. And everybody's paying attention and well, can I get 1%, can I get 2%, can I get 3%? You've seen, I've gotten conversion rates at 16%. I've had sales conversion rates as high as 30%.

The thing is that everybody's focusing on that. But one of the fastest ways to raise that number is to focus on the other 99% or the 97% or the 70% that aren't buying. You ask them why, just ask them why aren't you subscribing. Why aren't you watching this video all the way to the end? Why aren't you doing this?

Be real cool about it. Don't get all up in their face. But you'd be amazed at the information people will give you through an exit offer. Or the amount of money you can make by paying attention to them.

Conclusion

This is really just the tip of the iceberg when it comes to sales and conversion. I've given you 10 solid tips, trick and tools to increase sales and profits. There are lots more ways to increase sales and conversion on your website or blog.

The biggest thing I want you to take away from this book, you need to remember this is a process. Increasing your sales and profits using Tips, Tricks & Tools is something that takes place over time. It's something that you have to do and engage in.

Rarely will you ever be perfect out of the gate. I have one website where I truly believe that the headline that I got was divinely inspired. I think God threw me a bone because I was in a hard time in my life. This was right before I got fired from my job. God said, "Hey, here's a killer headline, Jim. Do something with it." And I did. And I've never been able to beat that particular headline.

The key here is really to do something. Go get results. Then make steady, gradual improvement so that you can get better results from the same or less marketing expense.

That's the part that's so exciting about increasing conversion. You can spend the same amount of money, time, energy and effort to generate traffic, to generate visitors, to generate eyeballs to look at your website. But by increasing the conversion rate you can geometrically improve and increase your profitability and what happens from that.

I hope to see you again very soon with more useful advice for improving your financial goals and lifestyle.

Jim Edwards

Williamsburg, Virginia

Now YOU Can Finally Discover The REAL WORLD Blueprint For Online Business Profits Today!

You can stop struggling and finally put your online business on the **solid foundation you need**, combined with **up-to-date monthly webinars of what's working now** in the world of Digital Marketing.

LIVE Monthly Training webinar with the newest strategies and nuts & bolts mechanics to keep you on the cutting edge of what's working in online sales...

LIVE Q&A Monthly webinar where you get YOUR questions answered by me personally and you'll get everything you need to keep your business running full-steam-ahead...

- **Get started immediately on your "***Fast-Track* Video Coaching" Training**

Jim's **"TheNetReporter"** is the quickest and easiest way for you to get on the *FASTTRACK* to success. For a **FREE Video with all the details** go to:

www.TheNetReporter.com

NOTES:

NOTES

NOTES: